BIGGEST NAMES IN SPORTS

FERNANDO TATÍS JR.

BASEBALL STAR

by Todd Kortemeier

FOCUS READERS®

NAVIGATOR

WWW.FOCUSREADERS.COM

Focus Readers is distributed by North Star Editions:
sales@northstareditions.com | 888-417-0195

Produced for Focus Readers by Red Line Editorial.

Photographs ©: Laurence Kesterson/AP Images, cover, 1; Andrew Dieb/Icon Sportswire, 4–5, 7; Matthew Pearce/Icon Sportswire, 9; David Seelig/Icon Sportswire, 10–11; Andrew Woolley/Four Seam Images/AP Images, 13, 15; Kevin Abele/Icon Sportswire, 16–17; Gregory Bull/AP Images, 19, 25, 27; Gene J. Puskar/AP Images, 21; Brian Rothmuller/Icon Sportswire, 22–23; Red Line Editorial, 29

Library of Congress Cataloging-in-Publication Data
Names: Kortemeier, Todd, 1986- author.
Title: Fernando Tatís Jr. : baseball star / Todd Kortemeier.
Description: Lake Elmo, MN : Focus Readers, [2023] | Series: Biggest names in sports | Includes index. | Audience: Grades 4-6
Identifiers: LCCN 2021055431 (print) | LCCN 2021055432 (ebook) | ISBN 9781637392607 (hardcover) | ISBN 9781637393123 (paperback) | ISBN 9781637394137 (pdf) | ISBN 9781637393642 (ebook)
Subjects: LCSH: Tatis, Fernando, Jr., 1999---Juvenile literature. | Baseball players--United States--Biography--Juvenile literature. | Baseball players--Dominican Republic--Biography--Juvenile literature. | San Diego Padres (Baseball team : National League of Professional Baseball Clubs)--Juvenile literature.
Classification: LCC GV865.T27 K67 2023 (print) | LCC GV865.T27 (ebook) | DDC 796.357092 [B]--dc23
LC record available at https://lccn.loc.gov/2021055431
LC ebook record available at https://lccn.loc.gov/2021055432

Printed in the United States of America
Mankato, MN
082022

ABOUT THE AUTHOR

Todd Kortemeier is a sportswriter, author, and lifelong baseball fan who grew up idolizing Tony Gwynn and the San Diego Padres. He hopes to one day see a statue of Fernando Tatís alongside Gwynn's at Petco Park in San Diego. He now lives near Minneapolis with his wife and daughter.

TABLE OF CONTENTS

23

CHAPTER 1

CHANGING THE GAME

Fernando Tatís Jr. stood in the batter's box. The bases were loaded. He faced a count of three balls and no strikes. Tatís and the San Diego Padres led the Texas Rangers 10–3 in the eighth inning. The Padres were on their way to an easy victory. No one could have guessed that

Fernando Tatís Jr. hits a grand slam against the Texas Rangers in 2020.

Tatís was about to show how the game of baseball was changing.

Tatís got a fastball. He put his best swing on it. The ball soared deep into right field. The Rangers outfielder could only watch as the ball flew into the seats. It was a **grand slam**!

Tatís had just blasted his 11th home run of the 2020 season. San Diego now led Texas 14–3. But not everyone was happy. The Rangers manager was upset. The Rangers players were upset, too. Even the Padres manager shook his head.

Many people believed Tatís had broken one of the unwritten rules of baseball. These are not actual rules of the game.

Tatís celebrates with teammates after hitting a grand slam.

But they are guidelines that most players follow. For example, players usually don't swing at a 3–0 pitch if their team already has a big lead. Many people think it shows bad **sportsmanship**.

After the game, Tatís talked to reporters. He said he wasn't trying to embarrass the Rangers. He was just trying to do his best. He wanted to help his team win. Tatís hadn't even known that such an unwritten rule existed. He said he wouldn't do it again.

But other players and fans defended Tatís. For instance, many young players thought the unwritten rules didn't belong in baseball anymore. They said players should have fun. They also believed players should always do their best in any situation.

Playing hard all the time was one of the traits fans loved about Tatís. He had

Tatís turns a double play during a 2020 game against the Rangers.

been doing it since he was a kid. And he wasn't going to stop now that he was in the major leagues.

21

CHAPTER 2

EL NIÑO

Fernando Tatís Jr. was born on January 2, 1999. He grew up in San Pedro de Macorís, a city in the Dominican Republic. His father, Fernando Sr., didn't have much time to spend with his son. He had to work. Fernando Sr. played Major League Baseball (MLB).

Fernando Tatís Sr. plays in a 2001 game with the Montreal Expos.

Not surprisingly, Fernando Jr. grew up loving baseball. He started playing at the age of four. By the time he was 12, he was too good to play with kids his own age. So, he played on teams with older kids. For that reason, he picked up the

JUST GRAND

On April 23, 1999, Fernando Tatís Jr. was only three months old. On that day, Fernando Sr. was playing for the St. Louis Cardinals. In the third inning, he came to the plate with the bases loaded. He blasted a grand slam. Later in the same inning, he came to the plate again. Once again, the bases were loaded. And once again, Tatís hit a grand slam. He was the first player in MLB history to hit two grand slams in one inning.

Fernando Tatís Jr. makes a play during a 2017 game with the Fort Wayne TinCaps.

nickname "El Niño." That's Spanish for "The Kid."

In 2015, Fernando started getting attention from MLB teams. The Chicago White Sox signed him when he was only 16. But Fernando wasn't ready for the major leagues just yet. He would start in the **minor leagues** and work his way up.

Fernando didn't get a chance to show his skills to the White Sox. Before the season started, he was traded. Chicago sent him to the San Diego Padres.

During the 2016 minor league season, Fernando showed flashes of talent. But he really took off in 2017. That season, he slugged 22 home runs and stole 32 bases. He was still young, though, and he had plenty of things to work on. For example, he struck out a lot. He also made too many **errors** at shortstop.

Heading into the 2018 season, Tatís was ranked as one of the top **prospects**

Fernando Tatís Jr. swings for the fences during a minor league game in 2017.

in minor league baseball. Unfortunately, a thumb injury ended his season early. But that didn't derail his path to MLB for long.

2019
ARZ
JR.

CHAPTER 3

THE TOP PROSPECT

Many baseball players go back home when the season ends. After the 2018 minor league season, Fernando Tatís Jr. did the same. However, he didn't take a break. He played with his hometown team, Estrellas Orientales. His father was the team's manager.

Tatís takes a swing during a 2019 spring training game.

During one postseason game, Tatís hit the winning home run. To celebrate, he flipped his bat high into the air. Tatís went on to help Estrellas win their first championship in 51 years.

Padres fans hoped Tatís could do for them what he did for Estrellas. The Padres had never won a championship in their 50-year history. Fans saw Tatís as the player who could change that.

Heading into 2019, Tatís was the No. 2 prospect in all of baseball. However, he was still just 20 years old. Few people expected him to be ready for the big leagues. Tatís proved them wrong. The Padres added Tatís to their Opening Day

Tatís runs to first base for his first major league hit.

roster. The young shortstop skipped an entire level of the minor leagues.

A packed stadium of Padres fans stood and roared when he was introduced at the 2019 season opener. And Tatís showed that he belonged. In his first career at-bat, Tatís got a hit off ace pitcher Madison Bumgarner. Later in the game, Tatís dropped down a bunt. He used his blazing speed to get an infield single.

The highlights kept coming for El Niño. In a June game, Tatís led a six-run **comeback** against the Colorado Rockies. Tatís got the first hit of the ninth inning. Later in the inning, he lined a hit to center field to send home the tying run.

In August, Tatís leaped impossibly high to snare a line drive. Not even Tatís thought he was going to catch it. Fans got used to seeing him do the impossible. It seemed like nothing could

Tatís dives into home plate during a 2019 game against the Pittsburgh Pirates.

slow down Tatís. However, a back injury ended his **rookie** season after 84 games. Tatís ended the year with a .317 batting average and 22 homers. Unfortunately, Padres fans would have to wait even longer than they expected to see their superstar again.

SAN DIEGO

CHAPTER 4

THE FACE OF BASEBALL

Padres fans hoped for big things in 2020. But those hopes had to wait. The season was delayed because of the COVID-19 **pandemic**. Teams didn't start playing until July. The season lasted just 60 games instead of 162. And fans couldn't attend the games. So, games took place in empty stadiums.

Tatís takes a swing during the shortened 2020 season.

Padres fans had to watch on TV as Fernando Tatís Jr. took the next steps in his career. He finished second in the league in home runs. More importantly, the Padres made it to the postseason. In the first round, they faced the St. Louis Cardinals. Tatís was quiet in Game 1, and the Padres lost. In Game 2, San Diego

CHOP IT UP

In 2019, the Padres started a unique celebration. After a player made a big hit, he would turn back toward the dugout. Then he would make a chopping motion. Tatís brought this celebration from his team in the Dominican Republic. It was a nod to Dominican sugarcane workers who cut down stalks all day. Tatís's teammates loved it.

Tatís flips his bat after hitting a home run against the St. Louis Cardinals during the 2020 postseason.

fell behind 6–2. But in the sixth inning, Tatís came to the plate with two runners on base. He hammered the ball over the left-field fence to make the score 6–5.

By the next inning, the Padres had a one-run lead. Tatís stepped to the plate with a runner on base. This time, he sent a deep shot to right field. As the ball soared out of the park, Tatís turned to his own dugout. He flipped the bat as he pumped up his teammates. The Padres went on to win the game and the series.

San Diego's postseason run ended in the next round. But fans had high hopes for the future. Tatís had become one of the most popular players in baseball. Before the season started, the Padres signed him to a new 14-year contract. At $340 million, it was the third-largest contract in MLB history.

Tatís hustles to first base during a game in 2021.

In 2021, Tatís proved he was worth it. He led the league with 42 home runs. He was also voted to start his first All-Star Game. All that was left was delivering a World Series title to San Diego.

FERNANDO TATÍS JR.

- Height: 6 feet 3 inches (190 cm)
- Weight: 217 pounds (98 kg)
- Birth date: January 2, 1999
- Birthplace: San Pedro de Macorís, Dominican Republic
- Minor league teams: AZL Padres (2016); Tri-City Dust Devils (2016); Fort Wayne TinCaps (2017); San Antonio Missions (2017–18); Estrellas Orientales (2017–19)
- MLB team: San Diego Padres (2019–)
- Major awards: Silver Slugger Award (2020); MLB All-Star (2021)

Pasco
San Diego
Fort Wayne
San Antonio
Peoria
San Pedro de Macorís

FOCUS ON
FERNANDO TATÍS JR.

Write your answers on a separate piece of paper.

1. Write a sentence that describes the key ideas from Chapter 1.
2. Do you think Tatís should have swung on a 3–0 pitch when his team had a big lead? Why or why not?
3. Which team did Tatís's father manage?
    - **A.** San Diego Padres
    - **B.** Chicago White Sox
    - **C.** Estrellas Orientales
4. Why did the White Sox trade Tatís before he had ever played a game?
    - **A.** It was too early to tell whether Tatís would be a star.
    - **B.** The other White Sox players refused to play with Tatís.
    - **C.** The team knew Tatís would break baseball's unwritten rules.

Answer key on page 32.

GLOSSARY

comeback
A situation where a team is losing but ends up winning the game.

errors
Mistakes by a player who should have been able to get an out or stop a runner from advancing.

grand slam
A home run with the bases loaded.

minor leagues
The lower levels of a sport.

pandemic
A disease that spreads quickly around the world.

prospects
Players who are likely to be successful in the future.

rookie
A professional athlete in his or her first year.

roster
The list of players on a team.

sportsmanship
Competing in a fair and respectful way.

TO LEARN MORE

BOOKS

Chandler, Matt. *Fernando Tatís Jr.: Big-Time Hitter.* North Mankato, MN: Capstone Press, 2022.

Gigliotti, Jim. *San Diego Padres*. Mankato, MN: The Child's World, 2019.

Kortemeier, Todd. *Manny Machado: Baseball Superstar.* Mendota Heights, MN: Press Room Editions, 2019.

NOTE TO EDUCATORS

Visit **www.focusreaders.com** to find lesson plans, activities, links, and other resources related to this title.

INDEX

Answer Key: 1. Answers will vary; **2.** Answers will vary; **3.** C; **4.** A